Stepping Stories to Bigger Faith for Little People

A Collection of Family Devotions

Written by Joyce Herzog
Illustrated by Marvin Jarboe

GReenLeaf
P·R·E·S·S

© Joyce Herzog, 1995
Published by
Greenleaf Books, LLC
3761 Highway 109N, Unit D, Lebanon, TN 37087
First Edition
Second Printing November 1998

Internet: www.greenleafpress.com
3761 Highway 109 N., Unit D
Lebanon, TN 37087
615-449-1617

Preface

Stepping Stones
To Bigger Faith For Little People
A Collection of Family Devotions

A few years ago, when I knew I was to become a foster parent, I looked for a devotional to use with a three to eight year old. I found children's Bible stories, which were presented as fairy tales, and stories about Billy and Susie and their grandparents, which were pleasant, but fairly meaningless. I could not find devotions which put Biblical truths into language easy enough for a child to read and understand. I wrote these to meet that need. After teaching many children over the years, I have discovered that they do not need watered down truth. They respond very well to a simple presentation of mature concepts.

I recommend that you use this book as a family devotional. The devotions open doors for meaningful discussion which will benefit every member of the family. It is my prayer that these may be a blessing to you and your family, that through them, many may be won for God's Kingdom, and all may strengthen their spiritual walk.

Joyce Herzog

From Head to Heart To Hands

How to Use This Book

These passages are too meaty to read a new one every day. It is better to concentrate on the concept of one devotion through an entire week. Both children and adults need time to assimilate ideas and make them their own. There are forty devotions, enough for one a week for a school year. Reread the week's devotion every day or two. Talk about the concept and how you are striving to put it into your own life. Choose one related activity from the following list each day to do with your family.

- Read the Bible verse in two additional translations.

- State the meaning of the Bible verse in your own words.

- Trace and color the picture.

- Memorize the Bible verse.

- Retell the devotion in your own words.

- Copy the Bible verse in your neatest writing.

- Teach the lesson to a friend.

- Make a poster of the Bible verse.

- Act out the devotion.

- Tell how you plan to put the lesson into action.

- Copy the Bible verse in pen and ink and send it to a friend or relative.

- Find another verse in scripture that confirms the message.

- Sing the Bible verse to God using a new melody.

- Give another illustration of the lesson.

- Make a collage using words and pictures from the lesson.

- Name one person in scripture you think learned this lesson. Tell why.

- Name one person in scripture you think did not learn this lesson. Tell why.

- Tell how the message has affected your life.

- Write or say a prayer of thanksgiving and praise to God for teaching you this lesson.

- Use another art form (clay, painting, diorama, etc.) to illustrate the lesson.

- Print the Bible verse in decorative writing.

- Make a banner of the Bible verse.

- Copy the Bible verse onto a postcard and mail it to someone you love.

- Invite a friend or family to dinner and read the devotion again. Show them some of your projects or tell them how the verse affected you.

Table Of Contents

But God commendeth His love toward us,
in that, while we were yet sinners,
Christ died for us.
Romans 5:8

While Yet Sinners!

When your baby brother is happy and laughing, it is easy to show him your love. You may tickle him or give him a toy or hug him. But when he has been crying for a long time and you are tired of hearing him, it may be hard to love him and be nice to him — especially if you tried already and he just got madder.

God tried to show His love to us, too, at a hard time. He didn't wait for us to be good or quiet. He showed His love while we were still sinning and fighting against Him. And he didn't just give us a toy. He gave us the thing that was most special to Him — His own Son.

God loved you that much even when you weren't very lovable. Doesn't that make you want to hug Him back? You can hug Him in words. Just tell Jesus how much you love Him, and how special His love is to you.

For all have sinned,
and come short of the glory of God.
Romans 3:23

Far From Perfect

God designed us to be perfect, holy, and full of glory. And then gave us the freedom to choose our own way.

God didn't want us to be puppets on a string acting this way or that as the strings are pulled. How could He be happy if we obeyed Him only because we had no other choice? How could He be happy if we loved Him like a puppet only when He pulled our strings? He wants us to love Him because we choose it. But we have all used our freedom to turn from God's perfect way.

We have all sinned. None of us lives up to God's perfect design. Isn't it good that God doesn't leave us sitting there in our sin? He wants us to admit that we have sinned, but He doesn't stop there.

Read Romans 6:23 and know that God has not left us without an answer.

For the wages of sin is death; but the gift of God is eternal life through Jesus Christ Our Lord. — **King James Version**

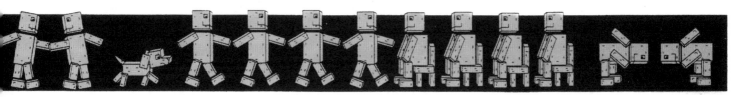

For the wages of sin is death; but the gift of God is eternal life through Jesus Christ Our Lord.
Romans 6:23

Eternal Life: God's Free Gift

Of your mom or dad has a job, the money they get for doing their work is called their wages. They earn their wages by doing what their boss wants.

When we sin, we do what the boss of the sin-world wants, and he pays us our wages. Our sin earns eternal death, being forever separated from God and His love.

We have already earned death because of the sin we have committed. But God is love and He has a gift for us that will replace what we have earned for ourselves. His gift is eternal life.

We didn't do anything to earn this free gift. We couldn't. It is ours for the taking — free; a gift of God.

We have, by sinning, earned the death penalty. But God's free gift is ready for us. Eternal life, living forever in the joy of being with God, is waiting for us. Reach out to God right now and take the free gift He has for you.

And Jesus said unto them, I am the bread of life:
he that cometh to me shall never hunger...
John 6:35a

Food for Life

God has a plan for you to live forever. He loves you so much He wants you to be his friend forever.

Ever since you were a little baby you have been eating. The food you eat gives your body what it needs to grow. We need food to live. But all the food in the world cannot help us grow unless we eat it. We must put it into our mouth and chew it and swallow it. Then our body knows how to use it to make us strong and tall.

Jesus says He is the Bread of Life. He is what we need to let us live forever. He is what we need to make us strong. He is our food. If we take Him into ourselves, He will live in us and let us live forever. But if we don't ask Him into us, He cannot help us grow.

Did you ask Jesus into your heart yet? If you did, He is still there and you will live forever in heaven. If you did not, think about it. Don't you want some of this food for life?

Thy Word is a lamp unto my feet,
and a light unto my path.
Psalm 119:105

A Light on the Path

God has given us a light for our walk through life.
Did you ever take a walk on a dark night with only a flashlight to light the path? A flashlight can not light up everything. If we shine it right in front of us, it will show us enough to take the next step safely. But if we shine it far away, we may not be able to see what is right next to us.

God says the Bible, His Word, will be a flashlight for our walk through life. And, like a flashlight, it will show us the next step that we must take. The Bible will not always show us what will happen many years ahead. It will not tell us what cereal to eat or what game to play. But it will show us one step at a time.

Can a flashlight light your path if it is sitting on a shelf at home? Can it light your path if you never turn it on? No, you must use it. And you must read God's Word if it is to light your path in life.

Are you walking in the dark today? Or are you using your flashlight, the Bible?

*If we confess our sins, He is faithful and just
to forgive us our sins, and to cleanse us
from all unrighteousness.*
I John 1:9

Washing Sins

When God looks at our sin, He sees it as dirt in our life that needs to be washed away. It makes Him sad to see the dirt. He thinks about how pretty we look to Him when we are clean and without sin.

We all sin. Before we were Christians it was easy to sin. Sometimes we didn't know, and sometimes we didn't care. Jesus died for all our sins. But God has a rule about sins:

God says when we sin we are to tell Him about it. He does not want us to pretend that we have not sinned. He even says that if we say we have not sinned we make Him a liar. He wants us to agree with Him that we have done wrong. And then He has a wonderful promise that goes along with this rule.

God says that when we tell Him about our sin, He will be faithful and fair and forgive us. He will also wash us clean. He doesn't say maybe. He doesn't say sometimes. He says He *will* forgive us and wash us clean.

He telleth the number of the stars;
He calleth them all by their names.
Psalm 147:4

Counting Stars

The stars shine in the sky at night. Have you ever looked at the sky on a clear summer night? The stars shine brightly and seem to twinkle at times. When you were little did you try to count them? Did you stop at 100? Or 500? Or did you finally give up? And there are many more stars that are too far away to be seen without a telescope.

But God, who made the stars, has counted them — and even named each one. Isn't that too wonderful to imagine? And can you think that if God counts and names even the stars in the sky He could forget one of His children here? No! He knows each one of us. He keeps track of us and calls us by name.

It is good to know that God is so great – He sees all the stars; and He is so loving He cares for each one. It is even more wonderful to know that God knows and cares for me!

And looking upon Jesus as He walked,
He saith, Behold the Lamb of God!
John 1:36

The Blood Of The Lamb

A long time ago, even before Jesus lived, God made a rule about sin. Sin made Him so sad that he told the people when they sinned, the blood of a spotless lamb must be shed. He wanted them to think about their sins — and to try hard not to sin. For a while the people tried hard. But then they forgot. They killed a lamb and then sinned again. This made God even sadder. But he had another plan:

God sent His own Son, Jesus, to be the Lamb for everyone's sin. Jesus lived on the earth for a while. He told people about God's Love. Then He went to the cross to die. The Bible tells us that Jesus never sinned. He was like the spotless lamb. His blood was shed for us — to pay for our sins.

Jesus paid for your sin. But you must tell God you want it to count for you. Tell God you want the blood of Jesus to cover your sin.

Seeing ye have purified your souls in obeying the truth through the Spirit unto unfeigned love of the brethren, see that ye love one another with a pure heart fervently.
I Peter 1:22

Love Is Obedience

This verse tells us that God's Spirit gives us the power to obey the truth. After we obey the truth, then we will find that we have real love for our Christian brothers and sisters. But we may not be used to telling or showing love to others. We may not know how, or may be afraid to. The old feeling of jealousy and selfishness may still be in us.

Just like children, we must learn how to show God's love to each other. Start by looking at other Christians. Listen when they tell each other about God's love and their own love. Watch to see what good things they may do for each other. Think what nice things you'd like for someone to do for you — then do them for someone else. Listen, watch, think; then do.

It is not enough just to obey the truth. It is not enough to just feel love for our Christian friends. This verse tells us to be sure to show that love to them with a pure heart. That means we are not to do it for what we will get out of it, but just because of God's love.

It also says to do it fervently – that means to the very best of our ability – eagerly – with a smile.

I will both lay me down in peace, and sleep:
for thou, Lord, only makest me dwell in safety.
Psalm 4:8

Peaceful Sleep

Have you ever had trouble going to sleep? Did you think there were monsters under the bed? Or bears in the air? Did you call Mom for a glass of water? Or one more good night kiss?

God says we don't have to be afraid any more. We can just lay down in peace and sleep. Even if we are all alone we don't have to worry; God will be with us all night. He will keep us safe.

Next time you go to bed, think about God being with you. He is your Protector. If you hear a creaky noise you may want to think that Jesus is coming to say good night. And it will help you remember to talk to Him before you go to sleep.

Afraid at night? Not any more! You have a Protector. Now you can sleep in peace.

If any of you lack wisdom, let him ask of God,
that giveth to all men liberally, and upbraideth
not; and it shall be given him.
James 1:5

Wisdom For The Asking!

Have you ever tried to decide something that seemed very hard to do? Like, how can I stop fighting with my brother; or should I live with my mom or my dad? It takes wisdom to know what to do at times like that. It may take more wisdom than we have. We may not be wise enough.

But God has the answer to that problem. God says if we lack wisdom, we only need to ask Him for it, and He will give it to us. We may be afraid to ask. We may think we have to decide alone. We may wonder if God will be angry with us. But the Bible says God gives to all men generously without making them feel bad.

Wisdom is ours. It is right at the tip of our tongue. We only have to ask God. He will give it to us.

Why do we have to ask? God knows what we need; why doesn't He just give it to us? God wants us to be willing to show Him that He is important to us; to show Him that we know we need Him. God wants the joy of giving us what we need; but He also wants the fellowship of talking with us. He wants us to know that the answer comes from Him.

Are you confused? Uncertain about what to do, or what to think? Ask God for wisdom. He will give it to you in love.

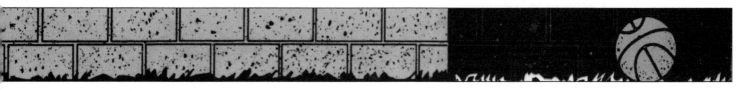

Be careful for nothing; but in every thing
by prayer and supplication with thanksgiving
let your requests be made known unto God.
Philippians 4:6

Don't Worry

Have you been a worrier? A worrier is someone who is always thinking that bad things may happen. Some people worry about things that have already happened, things that might happen, and many things that never will happen.

God says that a Christian should never worry. Worrying cannot keep something bad from happening. Nor can it undo something bad that has happened. Worrying can only make you sad and make others around you sad too.

God tells us to pray about everything, and not worry. We must talk to God and ask Him to take care of everything.

When we ask God to take care of something, we know we don't need to worry. We know He will answer our prayer. So we can thank Him right away for what He is going to do. God says when we do this we will feel peaceful. Worry brings sadness. Prayer and thankfulness bring peace. Why worry when you can pray?

In every thing give thanks: for this is the will of God
in Christ Jesus concerning you.
I Thessalonians 5:18

Thankful Because

Do you know what it means to be thankful? Remember that special present you had wanted for so long, that you got for Christmas, or your birthday? Remember how good it felt to have it at last? Did you thank someone for it?

Or maybe you almost had a bad accident, but nobody was hurt too badly. Or you did something very bad without thinking and someone forgave you. Or maybe your pet was very sick and got well again. You were thankful then because something good happened.

But God says we have another reason to be thankful – because it is His will for you. Because He wants you to be thankful no matter what happens. Even if it seems bad at first, thank God for it. God knows this will make you happier. And it will make it easier for Him to help you see how it may be good after all. If you are fighting God, you keep Him from showing you the good.

So be thankful – because God wants it for you.

Take heed unto thyself, and unto the doctrine;
continue in them: for in doing this thou shalt
both save thyself, and them that hear thee.
I Timothy 4:16

Watch What You Think

Watch what you do. And what you think. That's what God's Word says. We know we can often choose what we do. When we are playing, we can share our toys with our friends, or we can be selfish and play alone.

But did you ever think about watching what you think? God says we can. When we start to think something bad about a friend, we can choose to think something good instead. When we start to think of something mean to do, we can choose to think of something kind instead.

God says if we choose to think and do things that are right, He will bless us. That means He will give us happiness. And He will also do something very special. He will use us to help others. Then He will be pleased. They will be happy. And we will be happy. All that happiness because you chose to think and do what is right!

Watch what you think!

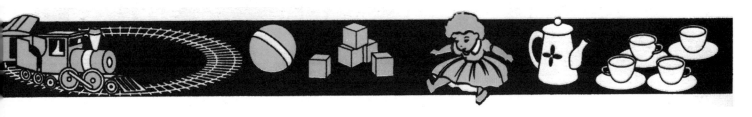

The law of the Lord is perfect, converting the soul: the testimony of the Lord is sure, making wise the simple. The statutes of the Lord are right, rejoicing the heart: the commandment of the Lord is pure, enlightening the eyes.
Psalm 19:7-8

Rules To Live By

God's Book, the Bible, is filled with rules about living in love. Some of these rules are in the Ten Commandments. But most of the rules are in other parts of the Bible. It may be hard to understand why there are so many rules.

When you were little, Mother probably said, "Don't touch the stove. It is hot!" That was the rule, wasn't it? Was it because mother was mean? No, she knew you were too young to know that stoves can be very hot. So she made the rule to protect you. She knew you would be happier if you didn't get burned. So she tried to help you keep the rule. She made the rule because she loved you.

God loves us too. He knows what will make us happy and what can hurt us. So God made rules to protect us and to lead us into happy living. If we obey these rules we will grow happier.

Do you want to be really happy? Then ask God to teach you His rules, and then to help you obey them.

*For it is God which worketh in you both to will and
to do of his good pleasure.*
Philippians 2:13

Wanting To Obey

God wants us to obey Him. He has given us rules for living a Christian life. These rules are to make us happier, and to please God. But we will only be happier if we obey the rules, and sometimes that is hard.

We can't always understand God's rules, because we are not as wise as He is and we do not know as much as He does. Sometimes the rules seem to be too hard to obey. Sometimes we cannot see the good that will come from obeying them. Or sometimes we just don't want to obey them.

But the Bible has happy news for us. It tells us that God will not only help us do what He wants; He will even help us **want** to obey Him.

Are you having trouble wanting to obey God? Tell Him about it. He has promised in His Word that He will help you want to obey Him.

*But thou art holy, O thou that inhabitest
the praises of Israel.*
Psalm 22:3

Praise The Lord!

If you have ever read the book in the Bible called the Psalms, you may have been surprised at how many times it tells us to praise the Lord! It must be important to be there so many times. The Bible tells us why it is so important. It says that God inhabits the praise of His people. Inhabits means lives in. God lives in praise. His house is built out of our praise. When we praise Him we are building His house.

What is praise? Think about the last time you did a really good job. Maybe you cleaned your room just right, or finally learned to spell a hard word. Did someone tell you what a good job you had done? They were praising you.

You can praise God by telling Him how much you love Him. Or you can tell Him how beautiful His world is. You can sing a song about His love. Or you can read parts of the Bible that praise Him.

You are building a house for God. Will it be a castle or a shack?

I know thy works, that thou art neither cold nor hot:
I would thou wert cold or hot. So then because thou art lukewarm,
and neither cold nor hot, I will spue thee out of my mouth.
Revelation 3:15-16

Hot Or Cold?

Many people talk about being on fire for Christ. That means they are really excited about living Jesus' way. They want to follow God's rules. They try to live in love.

Some other people may not care about God at all. We may say they give God a cold shoulder. They live their life as if there was no God.

And there are many who are somewhere in between. They believe in God. Maybe they even go to church. But the rest of the week they forget about God and His love.

There are three kinds of people. Which are you? God has something to say about these kinds of people. He says He wants us to be on fire for Him. But he would rather have us cold than somewhere in between. He says that those who are in between, neither hot nor cold, make Him sick; He will vomit them — cough them up and spit them out.

Ask God to help you be on fire for Him.

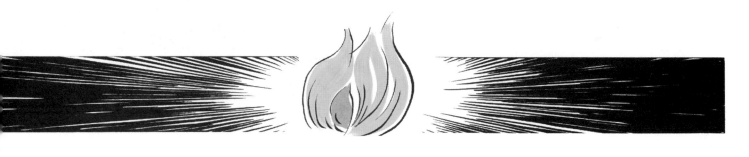

Let as many servants as are under the yoke
count their own masters worthy of all honour,
that the name of God and His doctrine be not blasphemed.
I Timothy 6:1

Worker For God

Are you a good worker? Or are you giving someone a chance to laugh at God?

People outside the church think Christians should be something special. Christians should not lie or cheat. And Christians should work hard; and be honest; and be happy all the time. They think Christians should be all those things. We know we are not perfect. But people outside the church think we should be. And when they see we are not, they laugh at God: "Ha Ha! Christians are no better than I am!"

Have you ever been laughed at? It didn't make you feel very good, did it? Think how God feels when people laugh at Him. He wants their love.

If you are a poor worker, people may laugh at God because of you. But if you are a hard worker, they may see you and say, "Maybe God is real after all."

Will people watching you laugh at God? Or will they see you and want to know your God?

Being confident of this very thing,
that he which hath begun a good work in you
will perform it until the day of Jesus Christ.
Philippians 1:6

Not Perfect Yet

Have you seen those colorful buttons and pins that tell of your faith. One of them has some letters that stand for words. The letters are P.B.P.G.I.N.F.W.M.Y. They stand for, "Please be Patient; God Is Not Finished With Me Yet."

When you asked Jesus into our heart, He came in. But that was only the beginning of God's work in you. When God looks at you now, He sees the perfect person you are going to be in heaven. He will help you to become that person.

You may feel bad one day about something you said or did. Or maybe you will feel bad about something you could have done, but didn't. This is God's way of telling you about something in your life that you need to change. When He shows you something to change, He will also give you the strength and power to change it. This is God's way of helping you to become perfect as He sees you can be.

The Lord upholdeth all that fall,
and raiseth up all those that be bowed down.
Psalm 145:14

Lifted Up

When you were little you fell down many times. Most of the time you probably just got right back up again. But sometimes you hurt too much. You scraped your knee — or you were tired; maybe you just sat there with your head down crying. Didn't it feel good when someone came and picked you up and hugged you? When you knew they loved you, somehow it didn't hurt as much.

When we are older, we don't fall down as much. But sometimes our spirits fall. We may feel very sad, even though we don't know why. Or we may feel bad because we can't do something we want to do — or because we did something we shouldn't have and were punished. When our spirits are very sad, there is Someone who wants to lift us up and bring hope and joy. That Someone is God.

God is always with you and He is always ready to lift you up when you are sad. Look up to Him. Let Him lift you up.

For God hath not given us the spirit of fear
but of power, and of love, and of a sound mind.
II Timothy 1:7

Life Without Fear

You have probably known someone filled with fear. They wouldn't play in the rain because they might catch a cold. They couldn't swim because they might drown. Their lives are controlled by fear.

Most of us are afraid of something. Maybe we are afraid of pain, or failing, or getting beat up. That fear keeps us from being happy and may keep us from doing some things we really want to do. It may keep us from doing what God wants us to do. It will for sure keep us from being the kind of person God wants us to be.

God's Word says that fear does not come from God. But He has given us the cure for fear. Fear is a coward. It runs from power, from love, and from sound thinking. When fear knocks at your door, tell it to go away. Choose instead to live with God's power. Ask God to fill you with His Love and that will scare fear away. The peace that you will feel knowing that fear is gone is the first step to the sound mind God has promised.

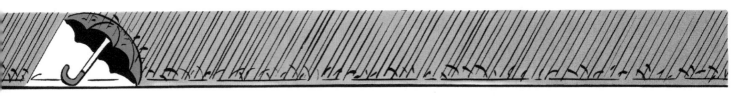

*Let this mind be in you, which was also
in Christ Jesus.*
Philippians 2:5

Christlike Attitude

God's Word tells us to have the attitude that Christ had. That is a special rule because it tells us first of all that we can choose what attitude we have. When we were little our attitude just sort of happened. When we were happy we were very happy, and we thought and acted happy. But when we were angry, watch out! We didn't choose to be angry. It just happened. But now we can learn to choose how we will think and feel, and the Bible tells us to copy Christ's attitude.

But to do that we must know what Christ's attitude was. Was He always loving and kind? Was He ever sad or angry? Did He ever feel all alone? I could tell you the answers. But I won't. The Bible tells all about Christ's life on earth — what He did, what He said, and even what He felt. But you can read. Christ's life is told in the Gospels; Matthew, Mark, Luke, and John. Ask God to teach you what you need to know. Then read about Christ.

It's not too late to begin to choose attitudes like Christ.

Praise ye the Lord. Praise God in His sanctuary:
praise Him in the firmament of His power.
Psalm 150:1

On His Sanctuary

We often praise God in a church sanctuary. When we go to church we sing songs of praise and we speak our praise.

But God says that is not enough. He says we are to praise Him in His sanctuary — in His mighty expanse. Did you ever think that all of the outdoors is His sanctuary? That means we praise Him wherever we are: On the way to school, at a campground, on top of a mountain, or in our backyard.

We need to meet other Christians in a church. But sometimes we need to meet God alone. The best place for that may sometimes be out under the sky. When we look around we can think about how very big God's world is. We can think about how pretty He made it. The wonder of His creation and the great love that made Him want to make it will lead us to praise Him. And that's what He tells us to do. Praise Him in His mighty expanse.

And now, little children, abide in Him;
that, when he shall appear, we may have confidence,
and not be ashamed before Him at his coming.
I John 2:28

Abide In Him

Once when I was little, Mom left me home with my brothers. While she was gone, we got into a cake she had baked for supper. Soon there was nothing left but crumbs on the counter. Then we heard her car pull in. We all ran and hid. We knew we had done wrong by eating the cake and we were ashamed and afraid of what she might do.

God has given us rules, and He leaves us to obey or disobey them. If we follow His way and live in love, we will be ready when He comes to the earth again. If we disobey, we will want to run and hide. But there will be nowhere to go. We will be ashamed, but we will have to face Him.

This verse tells us to abide in Him, so we will not have to hide in shame. Abide in Him means live in His love and try to do what will make Him happy.

If He came today could you run to Him smiling, knowing that you were living in His love? Or would you want to hide?

For every creature of God is good, and nothing to be refused,
if it be received with thanksgiving.
I Timothy 4:4

An Attitude Of Gratitude

Wow! This verse tells us that everything created by God is good! Not almost everything, but everything! The frog, the hippopotamus, the cripple. And you! Your nose, your body, your hair. And the you that thinks and feels and loves. You were created by God. You are good. Every child, every person was created by God. They are all good.

Did you ever reject someone because they looked different from you? Or because they acted different? Or did you ever not like yourself because of the way you looked or acted? God says you are good. They are good. And nothing is to be rejected. But there is an *if*. Nothing is to be rejected *if* it is received with gratitude. When you reject yourself or someone else, it is not because God wants you to. It is because you have forgotten to be grateful. You have forgotten to thank God.

Is there someone you don't like? Or something about yourself that you don't like? Thank God. Ask Him to change your attitude to gratitude.

But let every man prove his own work, and then shall he have rejoicing in himself alone, and not in another.
Galatians 6:4

Do Your Best

Mom has probably told you many times to do your best. Maybe your teacher said that too. Did you ever wonder why that is important?

Many times we look at our work; then we look at someone else's. If ours looks better we are happy. Maybe, to make ourselves happy we look at little brother's work – or the work of someone we know we can beat. Did you ever think about how the other person feels? Thinking your work is better, made you happy, but it makes the other person sad. The Bible tells us a better way.

The Bible says just to do your best. Then you will be satisfied because you know you've done as well as you can. So you won't need to compare yourself with others.

Do you find yourself looking for someone who doesn't do well so that your work looks good? Maybe you're not really doing your best. Is less than your best really good enough? Talk to God about it.

And whatsoever ye do, do it heartily, as to the Lord, and not unto men; Knowing that of the Lord ye shall receive the reward of the inheritance: for ye serve the Lord Christ.
Colossians 3:23-24

Jesus Our Boss!

When you do your schoolwork or your chores around the house, have you ever thought that you have a boss — an employer who hired you? You may not get money for what you do. Do you think you would work harder and do better if you knew your boss would pay more for work well done? The Bible tells us that we do have a boss who will reward us according to what we do. Our boss is Jesus!

Whatever we do, when we play and when we work, it is important to Jesus. He wants us to do our best; to be honest and loving. He wants us to always work as if He is our boss. Everything we say and do and think is important because Jesus loves us. We should always do our best to make Him happy and show Him that we love Him.

Have you been a lazy worker? Ask God to forgive you, and start right now to work for Jesus.

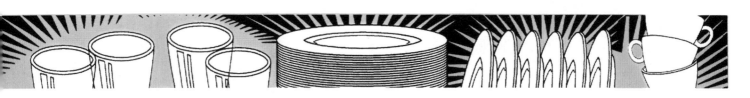

The Lord is not slack concerning His promise, as some men count slackness; but is long suffering to us-ward, not willing that any should perish, but that all should come to repentance.
II Peter 3:9

God Is Waiting

It was many years ago that Jesus promised to return; before we were alive. We may think He should have come a long time ago, or that He should come today.

But this verse tells us why He has not come yet. He does not want anyone to perish in hell and He is giving us time to repent. You have read in this book that you must tell God about your sins and ask Him to forgive you, so that you will live forever in heaven with God. Maybe you have heard about it in church. But have you done anything about it?

God is waiting. If you have not asked God to forgive your sins and give you life forever with Him, you may want to do it now.

If you have been forgiven, maybe God is waiting for you to tell your friends so they may live forever too.

God is giving you more time. What are you doing with it?

*Keep yourselves in the love of God, looking for the mercy of our
Lord Jesus Christ unto eternal life.*
Jude 1:21

Boundaries Of Love

Our life is filled with boundaries. Boundaries at school; if we go off the school lot we will get in trouble. Boundaries in a game of tag; if we get out of the boundaries we can not play. Boundaries in games; we lose a point if we get out of bounds. Boundaries at home, in the yard, around the block.

God has set up boundaries for us, too; but His boundary is not a line on the ground. It is a line of how to behave. We can get out of God's boundaries by disobeying His Word, by ignoring His will, or by not talking with Him and His people. Obedience and prayer are ways that we can keep in touch with God. When we are in touch with God, His love reaches us. But we can put up walls that stop God's love from reaching us. Some of the walls are hate, anger, sin, envy, greed, unbelief, and jealousy. God will not break down these walls we build unless we ask Him to.

Have you built a wall against God? Ask Him to help you tear it down.

Are you inside God's boundaries where His love reaches you? Reach out to Him. His love will surround you.

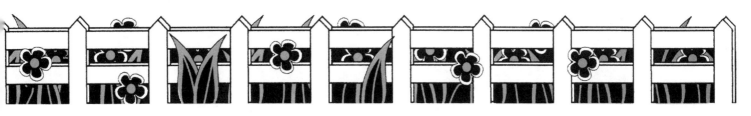

Rooted and built up in Him, and stablished in the faith, as ye have been taught, abounding therein with thanksgiving.
Colossians 2:7

Roots

The Bible compares us to flowers and tells us to let our roots grow deep into Jesus. For a flower, the soil is a source of food and strength, as well as a support. For us, Jesus is our source. We must set our roots still in the soil of Jesus and not pull them out, putting them here and there. For just as a flower, pulled and reset several times, will die; we, too, would wither and die if our roots could not stay and reach for food. If we let the roots soak up the food (that is, let ourselves soak up everything Jesus offers) we will grow to be strong and healthy Christians. And a beautiful flower will bloom in our life.

This verse tells that our lives will overflow with joy and thanksgiving to Jesus. Joy on our face is the bloom that everyone will see. Then, when they hear thanksgiving from our mouths given to Jesus as our source, they, too, will look to Him.

Take time today to sink your roots into Jesus. Tell Him you love Him. Read His Words to you in the Bible. Sing His praises. Worship Him with other Christians. Let Him feed you so that you will blossom.

*Give, and it shall be given unto you; good measure, pressed down,
and shaken together, and running over, shall men give into
your bosom. For with the same measure that ye mete withal
it shall be measured to you again.*

Luke 6:38

A Spoonful Of Love

God has given you many gifts. He gave you the trees and flowers, and the sky and sun. He gave you a family to love you and take care of you. And He gave you Jesus to die so that you might be free from the guilt of sin.

And now He says it is your turn to give. What can you give to God? You can give money to help others tell about Jesus' love. You can give time to help do God's work. And you can give love. You can love God. And you can show God's love to others, by loving them at all times.

God has a special rule about your giving. Think of a spoon. Fill it with ice cream. Taste it. Doesn't a spoonful of ice cream taste good? Now think of a tiny doll spoon. Fill it with ice cream. It doesn't hold much, does it? Taste it. Can you taste such a little bit of ice cream? No, there is not much there.

God says if you give someone a spoonful of love, He will fill that spoon as full as He can and give it back to you. He will press it down and shake it together and fill it until it over flows. But He must use the same size spoon you use.

Little children, keep yourselves from idols. Amen.
I John 5:21

God's Place

hat was on your mind today? What game to play? Who to play with? A problem at school?

What, or who, is special to you? Your new bike? Your best friend? The money in your bank?

None of these things are bad; but if they keep you so busy you don't have time for God, that is bad. Having special things or friends is not bad, unless they become so important you forget about God.

The Bible tells you to stay away from anything that might take God's place in your heart. If something, or someone, is keeping you from thinking about God, you should stay away from it.

God doesn't say this to make Him happy, or to make you sad. He knows that if you always think about these things they will bring you sadness. But, He knows if you think about Him and put Him first, you will be happier. And when you are happy everything will seem better.

So if there's something in your life that is keeping you from God, stay away from it.

This is the day which the Lord hath made;
we will rejoice and be glad in it.
Psalm 118:24

This Day The Lord Has Made!

Today isn't just any old day. It is the day the Lord made! And He made it just for you! Today is your day – a gift from God. What will you do with it?

You could wake up grumpy and cross and think it's going to be a bad day. And just thinking that may make it a bad day for you.

Or you can wake up and say "Good morning, Lord! Good morning, world! I'm going to have a good day today!" Then think of something to be glad about. Maybe the sun is shining, or maybe your world is being washed with rain. Maybe you have plans to visit a friend or special relative. Or maybe you can think of a surprise to make someone happy; it will make you happy too.

Early in the day, plan something to be glad about and you will find that you can rejoice and be glad in this day God has given you.

*...but this one thing I do, forgetting those things which are behind,
and reaching forth unto those things which are before, I press toward
the mark for the prize of the high calling of God in Christ Jesus.*
Philippians 3:13b and 14

A Brand New Day!

Each day the sun brings new light to a resting world. When it is dark at night we rest. Our bodies are tired from the things we have done. Perhaps our spirits are tired too — maybe they have been overworked by anger, tears, sorrow, or even by lots of joy. So the Lord gives another chance. When we sleep we put behind us the things of yesterday. When we wake up it is a brand new day.

Just as the food we ate yesterday will not fill our tummies today, so the events and accomplishments of yesterday will not carry us through today. We must determine to put yesterday behind ourselves and give our all to today. If there were sorrows and troubles yesterday, leave them there! If there was joy, remember it; but go on to find today's joy. Don't let yesterday's problems destroy today and don't let yesterday's accomplishments rob you of good works today by making you lazy.

Always reach for new goals, new strength in God; for the reward is the joy of knowing God's love through Jesus.

. . . yea, happy is that people, whose God is the Lord.
Psalm 144:15b

The Happiest People On Earth!

God made each one of us. He knows us better than we know ourselves. He knows what we need, because He made our needs. He made us to need His friendship.

God made in every person a need to be His friend – a need to receive God's love and to love God in return. No one can get away from that need. No one can be really happy until they receive and return God's love. People who turn away from God are never happy, because they still have a need to know and love God.

The people who make God their Lord are the people who are really happy because their need for God is filled.

You have read the lessons in this book. But what have you done about it? Have you prayed to God to help you live like the lessons teach? Do you read your Bible every day and ask what God wants you to learn? Have you asked God to be your Lord? Are you becoming more like Jesus? If you are, you are one of the happy people because you know God's love. If you haven't, what's stopping you?

For I know the thoughts that I think toward you, saith the Lord, thoughts of peace, and not of evil, to give you an expected end.
Jeremiah 29:11

Plans For Good

Sometimes we may look ahead to the future and wonder what it will hold for us. If we are feeling good that day we may think about happy plans and hope that our dreams will truly happen. But if things have gone wrong in our lives and we feel bad, we may think our future holds only bad things for us.

God tells us in His Word that we do not have to depend on our own feelings when we think about the future. He has made plans for our lives. Even before we were born God planned what He wanted for our lives. He knows what will bring us the most happiness and joy. And all of God's plans for us are plans for goodness and joy. God does not plan evil for His people.

Next time you think about the future you don't need to depend on your feelings. You can depend on God's Word. His plans for your future are good. You can depend on that.